Spiritual Warfare: Fighting to Win

D1603604

Spiritual Warfare: Fighting to Win

by
John MacArthur, Jr.

MOODY PRESS
CHICAGO

All Scripture quotations, unless noted otherwise, are from the *New Scofield Reference Bible,* King James Version. Copyright © 1967 by Oxford University Press, Inc. Reprinted by permission.

Library of Congress Cataloging in Publication Data

MacArthur, John, 1939-
    Spiritual warfare : fighting to win / by John MacArthur, Jr.
        p.   cm. — (John MacArthur's Bible studies)
    Includes indexes.
    ISBN 0-8024-5368-6
    1. Bible.   N.T.   Timothy. 1st I, 18-20—Criticism, interpretation,
etc.   I. Title.   II. Series: MacArthur, John, 1939-   Bible
studies.
BS2745.2.M34   1988
227'.8306—dc19   88-21582
                                        CIP

3 4 5 6 7 8 Printing/EP/Year 93 92 91

Printed in the United States of America

Contents

These Bible studies are taken from messages delivered by Pastor-Teacher John MacArthur, Jr., at Grace Community Church in Panorama City, California. The recorded messages themselves may be purchased as a series or individually. Please request the current price list by writing to:

WORD OF GRACE COMMUNICATIONS
P.O. Box 4000
Panorama City, CA 91412

Or call the following toll-free number:
1-800-55-GRACE

1
Fighting the Noble War—Part 1

Outline

Introduction
A. Timothy Received Exhortation from Paul
B. Timothy Faced Opposition from the Enemy

Lesson
I. The Preface to Spiritual Warfare
   A. A Description of the First Sinner (Ezek. 28:11-18)
      1. The perfection of Lucifer (vv.11-15a)
      2. The corruption of Lucifer (vv. 15b-18)
   B. A Disclosure of the First Sin (Isa. 14:12-15)
      1. The root of sin
      2. The response of God
II. The Participants in Spiritual Warfare
   A. Fallen Angels—Who They Are
      1. Their number
      2. Their status
   B. Fallen Angels—What They Do
      1. They oppose Christ
      2. They oppose Israel
      3. They oppose holy angels
      4. They oppose believers
III. The Program of Spiritual Warfare
   A. The Reality of Attack
   B. The Method of Attack
      1. How Satan attacks non-Christians
      2. How Satan attacks Christians
         a) Attacks upon individuals
            (1) Luke 22:31-32
            (2) 1 Peter 5:8

Introduction

In 1 Timothy 1:18-20 Paul says, "This charge I commit unto thee, son Timothy, according to the prophecies which pointed to thee, that thou by them mightest war a good warfare, holding faith and a good conscience, which some, having put away concerning faith, have made shipwreck; of whom are Hymenaeus and Alexander, whom I have delivered unto Satan, that they may learn not to blaspheme."

"War a good warfare" is better translated "fight a noble war." That key phrase gives us insight into Paul's challenge to Timothy, his son in the faith.

A. Timothy Received Exhortation from Paul

Paul called Timothy to fight a good war—to wage an excellent campaign. It is not a battle, skirmish, or brief fight; rather, it is a long-term war. He reminded Timothy that he was in a spiritual battle.

B. Timothy Faced Opposition from the Enemy

Paul left Timothy with the church in Ephesus to battle the enemy: false leaders in positions of prominence, power, and authority. Godliness was under attack. What Paul said to Timothy is instructive to all of us who are engaged in the same campaign.

The Primary Principle of Warfare

In Luke 14:31 Jesus presents a principle that has universal application to spiritual warfare: "What king, going to make war against

8

another king, sitteth not down first, and consulteth whether he is able with ten thousand to meet him that cometh against him with twenty thousand?" In other words, no king goes to war unless he understands the terms of battle, the power of his enemy, and the stakes of warfare. Likewise, we must evaluate our involvement in spiritual warfare.

Lesson

I. THE PREFACE TO SPIRITUAL WARFARE

A. A Description of the First Sinner (Ezek. 28:11-18)

In the beginning no war or rebellion existed; everything was in perfect harmony. No one opposed God's sovereign rule. No one voiced animosity toward anything that God expressed as His holy purpose and will. But then a disastrous event occurred. Ezekiel 28, a prophecy against the king of Tyre, helps us better understand the beginning of spiritual warfare.

1. The perfection of Lucifer (vv. 11-15a)

Verse 11 says, "The word of the Lord came unto me, saying, Son of man [a reference to Ezekiel], take up a lamentation upon the king of Tyre, and say unto him, Thus saith the Lord God: Thou sealest up the sum." The phrase "sealest up the sum" speaks of a perfect being— someone so complete that he possessed the seal of perfection.

Verse 12 goes on to say that this individual was "full of wisdom; and perfect in beauty." Obviously that cannot refer to a human being. No human is so perfect that further improvement is not possible. No human is full of wisdom or perfect in beauty.

Verse 13 says, "Thou hast been in Eden, the garden of God." This prophecy obviously goes beyond the king of Tyre. Rather, it is an indirect reference to the serpent —the adversary who was in the Garden of Eden.

9

Verse 13 continues, "Every precious stone was thy covering, the sardius, topaz, and the diamond, the beryl, the onyx, and the jasper, the sapphire, the emerald, and the carbuncle, and gold; the workmanship of thy timbrels [tambourines] and of thy flutes was prepared in thee." Apparently music heralded the birth of this marvelous angel.

Verse 14 addresses him as "the anointed cherub that covereth." God designed the Ark of the Covenant with two angels—one on each side, spreading their wings over the mercy seat. These angels were called "covering cherubs." They represented the angels associated with God's holiness, covering the place where atonement was made between God and man by the sprinkling of blood. These sacred angels were related to Lucifer, who was called "the anointed cherub that covereth"—the highest angelic creature caring for the glory and holiness of God.

Verse 14 continues, "I [God] have set thee so." God created angels in order of rank. There are angels and archangels, cherubim and seraphim, rulers, principalities, and powers. Those terms indicate that God designed an angelic network to carry out His bidding. Here, then, was an angel of supreme rank, created by God to be the anointed cherub.

Verse 14 says, "Thou wast upon the holy mountain of God; thou hast walked up and down in the midst of the stones of fire." This angel dwells with God upon the "holy mountain," which is heaven. "Stones of fire" refers to the holy ground upon which the throne of God was placed. Verse 15 summarizes, "Thou wast perfect in thy ways from the day that thou wast created."

2. The corruption of Lucifer (vv. 15b-18)

However, that was true only "till iniquity was found in thee" (v. 15). This disastrous event marks the beginning of spiritual warfare. Satan established himself against God.

Verses 16-17 continue the description of Satan's iniquity. God proclaimed, "Thou hast sinned; therefore, I will cast thee as profane out of the mountain of God, and I will destroy thee, O covering cherub, from the midst of the stones of fire. Thine heart was lifted up because of thy beauty; thou hast corrupted thy wisdom by reason of thy brightness." In other words, Satan's perfection was the cause of his corruption. The phrase "thine heart was lifted up" indicates that this sin originated from within Satan. We do not know how the sin came from within Satan, but it did.

In verse 18 God responds to Satan's sin: "Thou hast defiled thy sanctuaries by the multitude of thine iniquities, by the iniquity of thy merchandise; therefore will I bring . . . thee to ashes upon the earth in the sight of all them that behold thee." Because of his sin, God cast Satan out of heaven to be eventually destroyed.

B. A Disclosure of the First Sin (Isa. 14:12-15)

To determine the identity of the first sin, we turn to Isaiah, who described it in the midst of the prophesied destruction of Babylon. As in the case of Ezekiel's prophecy against Tyre, this prophecy indicates that there was a greater power behind Babylon. That power is identified in Isaiah 14:12: "How art thou fallen from heaven, O Lucifer, son of the morning!" The name *Lucifer* means "daystar" or "son of the morning." The phrase "how art thou fallen" is reminiscent of Luke 10:18, where Jesus says, "I beheld Satan as lightning fall from heaven."

1. The root of sin

Verses 12-14 say, "How art thou cut down to the ground, who didst weaken the nations! For thou hast said in thine heart, I will ascend into heaven, I will exalt my throne above the stars of God; I will sit also upon the mount of the congregation, in the sides of the north, I will ascend above the heights of the clouds, I will be like the Most High." Notice that the statement "I will" is repeated three times in verse 13 and two times in verse 14.

Lucifer's problem was pride. He was so close to God that he became jealous and sought to be equal to God.

The phrase "thou hast said in thine heart" (v. 13) indicates that sin comes from the heart, not from the environment. Satan was created in a perfect environment, yet sin came from within him. Satan in a sense invented pride. His pride produced discontentment, which led to his desire to be equal with God. Not satisfied to be an angel, he said, "*I will* ascend into heaven, *I will* exalt my throne above the stars of God; *I will* sit also upon the mount of the congregation" (emphasis added). The mount represents the place where God sits to meet and give counsel.

In verse 14 Satan says, "I will ascend above the heights of the clouds." In other words, Satan sought to surpass the height of God's glory—to be like God Himself. Pride caused spiritual warfare.

2. The response of God

God responds to Satan's sin in verse 15: "Thou shalt be brought down to sheol, to the sides of the pit." Satan's rebellion will ultimately bring his destruction.

II. THE PARTICIPANTS IN SPIRITUAL WARFARE

Revelation 12:3 says, "There appeared another wonder in heaven; and, behold, a great red dragon, having seven heads and ten horns, and seven crowns upon his heads." The dragon represents Satan at the helm of an anti-God, one-world government. The ten horns picture him as the supreme ruler of the final confederacy of nations, described in Daniel 7 as a revived Roman Empire that will pit itself against Christ.

A. Fallen Angels—Who They Are

1. Their number

Revelation 12:4 tells us that Satan did not fall alone: "His tail drew the third part of the stars of heaven and did cast them to the earth." When Satan fell, he drew with him one-third of the angelic host. Angels do not procreate or die. They live forever either in the domain of God or in the domain of Satan. There are as many angels today as there were the day God created them. According to our text, one-third of the angels went with Satan in his fall, and two-thirds remained with God.

Satan is not alone in cosmic warfare. He is tremendously powerful. Although he has great influence in the world, is able to control the souls of men, and is the force behind anti-God activities worldwide, he is not omnipresent. But his work is enhanced because a third of the angelic host is with him.

How many angels exist? We don't know. Revelation 5:11, speaking of heavenly angels alone, says there are "ten thousand times ten thousand" and "thousands of thousands," which in Greek is the greatest expression of numeration. We do not know how many there are, but a third of them followed Satan.

2. Their status

Some fallen angels are bound in "everlasting chains" (Jude 6). I believe those are angels who sinned at the time of the Flood in Genesis 6:1-7. Because they cohabited with mankind, producing a half-breed race, God drowned their offspring in the Flood and bound the angels with chains.

Other demons are bound temporarily. In Luke 8:31 the demons at Gadara beseech Christ "that he would not command them to go out into the deep." Perhaps God has put more and more demons into that pit throughout redemptive history. According to Revelation 9:2, some demons will be released during the Tribulation. But the demons in everlasting chains will remain bound.

Satan started with a third of the angels. Some are in everlasting chains; some are in temporary chains. The rest are with Satan, who opposes God and His holy angels.

13

B. Fallen Angels—What They Do

What are the specific targets of these angelic beings now known as demons?

1. They oppose Christ

Revelation 12:1 says, "There appeared a great wonder in heaven—a woman clothed with the sun, and moon under her feet, and upon her head a crown of twelve stars." Typical of the imagery in Revelation, the woman is Israel, the sun and the moon refer to Jacob and Rachel, and the twelve stars are Jacob's twelve sons (cf. Gen. 37:9).

Verse 2 says, "She, being with child, cried, travailing in birth, and pained to be delivered." The woman is about to bring forth a child who is the Messiah, the Lord Jesus Christ.

Verse 5 says, "She brought forth a male child, who was to rule all nations with a rod of iron [an obvious reference to Christ]; and her child was caught up unto God, and to his throne." Meanwhile, Satan gathers his forces: "The dragon stood before the woman who was ready to be delivered, to devour her child as soon as it was born" (v. 4). Satan has always fought the Messiah, which is why he tried to destroy the Christ child (cf. Matt. 2:16-18).

Today Satan fights against the work of Christ in His church. He will fight against Christ when He returns and will do so until he is cast into the lake of fire.

2. They oppose Israel

Verse 6 gives us the focal point of the battle during the time of the Tribulation: "The woman fled into the wilderness." That takes place during the last three-and-a-half years of the Tribulation, which is the period after the rapture and before the second coming of Christ. A holocaust will exist on earth as Satan attacks Israel. But God will supernaturally protect her.

3. They oppose holy angels

During the war on earth, "there was war in heaven; Michael and his angels fought against the dragon, and the dragon fought and his angels" (v. 7). That is another element of the warfare. God battles against Satan. But it is also Satan and his angels battling against God and His angels—the chief of them being Michael.

Scripture teaches that this battle is not relegated merely to the future. In Jude 9 Michael contends with Satan for the body of Moses. Even in the time of Moses, Michael and the devil were at war.

4. They oppose believers

Eventually the Tribulation battle filters down to believers. Verse 17 says that "the dragon was angry with the woman, and went to make war with the remnant of her seed, who keep the commandments of God, and have the testimony of Jesus Christ." During the Great Tribulation Satan increases his effort to thwart the plan of God. Therefore, in addition to his attack on Israel, Satan now attacks believers. Satan has always attacked the people of God and will continue to do so during this period. But God will preserve His people.

The war began between God and Satan. Next, war began between the holy angels and the fallen angels. The warfare involves those who know Jesus Christ—"who keep the commandments of God"—and those who do not know Him. Similarly, those saved during the Tribulation are also in the warfare. The lines are clearly drawn. On one side are Satan, fallen angels, and ungodly men; on the other side are God, holy angels, and the redeemed.

Satan Attacks God Through Men

Satan hates God. Therefore he hates those who bring glory to God. Our victories and defeats reflect on the God we serve and represent. When we are defeated, we have allowed Satan to attack God.

When we are victorious, we have defeated Satan in his attempt to attack God. Christians become involved in spiritual warfare because Satan wants to thwart the work of God. He wants to destroy the church because he hates God, who is the author of the church. The issue is God. We're simply instruments that Satan uses to attack God. When you fail to be what God would have you to be, you allow Satan to strike a blow at God. But when you live as you ought, you defend God against such an attack.

When Jesus cleaned out the Temple with a whip, He said, "It is written, My house shall be called the house of prayer, but ye have made it a den of thieves" (Matt. 21:13). Christ defended the glory of God. And that's what we're called to do.

III. THE PROGRAM OF SPIRITUAL WARFARE

A. The Reality of Attack

Some of you may say, "I don't see a battle." Maybe that's because you have deserted the battlefield.

It's appalling how many Christians live a trivia-oriented life. They don't know about the warfare because they haven't been in the battle. They are not courageous soldiers; they do not fight a noble war.

Paul said to Timothy, "Thou, therefore, endure hardness, as a good soldier of Jesus Christ. No man that warreth entangleth himself with the affairs of this life, that he may please him who hath chosen him to be a soldier" (2 Tim. 2:3-4). We're to expect to suffer hardship. We're to expect to be cut off from civilian affairs. We're to expect to do whatever we have to for the One who called us to be a soldier.

I was reminded of the spiritual war that surrounds us when I entered a room where there was a demon-possessed girl. Voices out of her screamed, "Get him out of here! Get him out of here! Not him, not him!" I realized the demons knew whose side I was on. That terrifying realization was soon replaced by a calm feeling. The demons understood where I stood.

16

One man who I spent six to eight months discipling left to attend a church that didn't teach the Scriptures. Later he attended an apostate seminary and became a rector in a church with unbiblical doctrines. I know from experience that we're in a war. And the battle isn't merely on an intellectual level; it goes much deeper.

B. The Method of Attack

How does Satan attack the church and the advance of God's kingdom?

1. How Satan attacks non-Christians

Second Corinthians 4:3 says, "If our gospel be hidden it is hidden to them that are lost." If the gospel is hidden, if the Word of God is dishonestly presented, or if the truth is held back, the ones who suffer are the lost.

Verse 4 says, "The god of this age [Satan] hath blinded the minds of them who believe not, lest the light of the glorious gospel of Christ, who is the image of God, should shine unto them." Satan does not want the gospel to shine because Christ is the image of God. The gospel reveals God, and Satan does not want men to see God's glory. Satan and his hosts blind the minds of the ungodly through various means.

a) Through ignorance

b) Through unbelief

c) Through the bad testimony of those who call themselves Christians

d) Through lies and false religion

e) Through a love of sin

f) Through fleshly gratification

More than Satan hates the ungodly he hates the glory of God, which is manifested in the face of Jesus Christ.

Because he desires to have more glory than God, Satan seeks to blind unbelievers. Yet while Satan continues to attack, God graciously gives light to the unsaved so that they might believe.

2. How Satan attacks Christians

    a) Attacks upon individuals

        (1) Luke 22:31-32—Christ said to Peter, "Simon, Simon, behold, Satan hath desired to have you, that he may sift you as wheat; but I have prayed for thee, that thy faith fail not. And when thou art converted [recovered], strengthen thy brethren." Those verses give us assurance that when Satan comes to destroy us, our high priest, Jesus Christ, prays that our faith will not fail. We need to be aware that Satan wants to fragment our lives and shake our confidence in God.

        (2) 1 Peter 5:8—Peter said, "Be sober [know your priorities], be vigilant [have your eyes opened, be aware], because your adversary, the devil, like a roaring lion walketh about, seeking whom he may devour." Satan tries to devour Christians.

    b) Attacks upon families

        The family is the unit God has designed to pass righteousness from this generation to the next. Therefore it is no surprise that Satan attacks the family.

        (1) A divine plan

            We gain insight into his method of attack in 1 Corinthians 7. Verse 3 says, "Let the husband render unto the wife her due; and likewise also, the wife unto the husband." In other words, husband and wife are to physically satisfy one another, for that is part of the marriage relationship. To further emphasize the point, Paul said, "The wife hath not power of her own body . . . the husband hath not power of his own body" (v. 4). In marriage, your body belongs to your spouse

18

for the satisfaction of his or her needs. And that is by the design of God. A fulfilling physical relationship should be part of the love commitment in a marriage.

(2) A divine warning

Verse 5 says, "Defraud ye not one the other, except it be with consent for a time, that ye may give yourselves to fasting and prayer." Withholding physical relations should not be used as leverage against your partner, or as a way to express your anger and indifference. Rather, the physical relationship should be postponed only when both agree to do so for the purpose of prayer and fasting. After that period, Paul said to "come together again, that Satan tempt you not for your incontinency" (v. 5). The point is this: Satan will do everything he can to destroy a Christian marriage.

A couple invites satanic attack when they withhold physical relations from one another in a manner that is not biblical. This example is only an emblem of Satan's attack upon the family.

c) Attacks upon leaders

In 1 Timothy 3 Paul addresses the spiritual leadership. In verse 2 he describes a pastor as being blameless and a one-woman man. In verse 6 he says the pastor is not to be a novice—a new convert, someone who is not skilled in the things of the Word. Then he gave his reason: "lest being lifted up with pride he fall into the condemnation of the devil" (v. 6). The pride that condemned Satan will condemn anyone who is prematurely placed in a position of spiritual leadership. Verse 7 says, "He must have a good report of them who are outside, lest he fall into reproach and the snare of the devil."

More than any other, the pastor is the person the devil would like to catch in a trap. And he is often successful today in doing that. Satan blinds many pastors to what he's doing in the world. Even those who see his deceptiveness often believe they can play around in his domain. However, they find that he devours them, shredding their lives. Spiritual leadership falls into his traps through immorality, pride, and dictatorial authoritarianism.

d) Attack upon the truth

Beginning in 2 Corinthians 10, Paul writes about true and false apostles, and he defends himself against attack. In 11:13 Paul identifies his attackers: "For such are false apostles, deceitful workers, transforming themselves into the apostles of Christ." He goes on to say that Satan transforms himself into an angel of light and his ministers into ministers of righteousness (v. 14).

Satan attacks the truth by establishing false religious systems throughout the world. Worldwide Satan attracts people into such false religions. Preaching that denies the deity of Christ or the depravity (lostness) of man is part of this system. One man who claims to be an evangelical implies that everyone is automatically saved because Christ dwells in everyone. Such teaching denies personal responsibility for coming to Christ.

The Urgency of Exposing Error

Sometimes I shiver when I see the heresy being taught in the name of biblical truth. I could go through illustration after illustration. For instance, I read a booklet written by a man who claims to have visited hell on three occasions. Yet this man is held up as an astute teacher and bearer of the truth.

Recently I was asked to go to Argentina to address an encroaching doctrinal error. The conference planners rented the largest facility available in Buenos Aires so that four thousand pastors could be taught the Word of God in reference to this error. They asked me to come because these pastors needed to understand the deceitfulness of Satan. It was a privilege to talk to those pastors about the truth of God when they're being attacked by the lies of Satan. It isn't that they don't know what to believe; it's that they want help in answering this error and help in arming their people so they won't be deceived into joining.

IV. PROTECTION IN THE MIDST OF SPIRITUAL WARFARE

How do we fight effectively? Second Corinthians 10:4 says, "The weapons of our warfare are not carnal, but mighty through God to the pulling down of strongholds." We can topple the kingdom of Satan. We can cast down his pretensions. Every high thing that exalts itself against the knowledge of God can be torn down. We can bring every thought into captivity and obedience to Christ (v. 5).

The weapons of our warfare can be reduced to one item: obedience. Our weapons are not mystical. The weapons of our warfare are not human intellect, prowess, skill, or ingenuity. When we put on the armor of God, we begin with the belt of truthfulness—a commitment to fight on the basis of God's revealed truth (Eph. 6:14). We put on the breastplate of righteousness, which is His revealed righteousness (v. 14). Our feet are shod with the gospel of peace, revealed in His Word (v. 15). Our helmet is our hope of eternal salvation, and our sword is the Word of God (v. 17). God's Word is our only weapon, and it is not a fleshy weapon. When I attack the kingdom of darkness with my opinion, I go nowhere. But when I attack with the Word of God, things start falling in place. The Word of God has tremendous power. Obedience to the Word is our weapon in warfare. As we wield the sword of the Spirit through an obedient life, covered with the breastplate of righteousness and the shield of faith, we will be victorious. Formulas don't work. Spirituality is nothing more and nothing less than obedience to the Word of God. That is the only thing enabling us to effectively confront the kingdom of darkness.

In order to be victorious in spiritual warfare we must make a commitment to obedience. That's how we start to fight the noble war. Jesus' Great Commission is summed up in the phrase "teaching them to obey everything I have commanded you" (Matt. 28:20, NIV*). Life and victory are inextricably connected to obedience.

*New International Version.

God wants us, like Timothy, to fight the noble war in a noble manner. The key is obedience to the Word of God. Many of you are fighting a noble war. God has given you great victory, and you're bringing glory to His name. I praise God for that. But if you're not in the battle, may God help you through these studies to be where you should be.

Focusing on the Facts

1. Who was the supernatural behind-the-scenes force in Ezekiel 28 and Isaiah 14 (see pp. 9-12)?
2. Define the phrase "sealest up the sum" (Ezek. 28:12; see p. 9).
3. Who is the dragon in Revelation 12 (see p. 12)?
4. Is Satan omnipresent (see p. 13)?
5. What expression is used in the Bible to describe the numbers of angels (see p. 13)?
6. Are all the fallen angels presently bound in "everlasting chains" (see p. 13)?
7. Who is the "male child" in Revelation 12:5? How do you know (see p. 14)?
8. When does Israel flee into the wilderness (see p. 14)?
9. What does Satan do to the minds of the ungodly (2 Cor. 4:3-4; see p. 17)?
10. What has God designed to pass righteousness to the next generation (see p. 18)?
11. Name the person Satan would most like to see fall into sin (see p. 19).
12. Who is the source of all false teaching (2 Cor. 11:13-14; see p. 20)?
13. What is the believer's only weapon in spiritual warfare (see p. 21)?

Pondering the Principles

1. In Ezekiel 28:11-18 and Isaiah 14:12-15 Scripture records the first sin: pride. Satan demonstrated his pride by his proclamation of independence—"I will." His iniquity brought judgment upon him. Likewise, man has received the pronouncement of God's wrath because his sin has made him the enemy of God (Rom. 5:10). The source of all sin is pride. Pride is the desire for inde-

pendence from God. Ask God to help you take inventory of your heart to identify areas where you have failed to submit to Christ's lordship. If you are a parent, help your children to see the biblical necessity of submitting to authority (cf. Eph. 6:1-2; Rom. 13:1-7).

2. The term *angel* is mentioned in Scripture approximately 275 times. Even though Christ Himself affirmed the existence of angels (Matt. 18:10), many Christians doubt their existence. On the other hand, renewed interest in the occult has increased the worship of angels and other so-called "spirit beings." Start your own study of angelic beings by tracing the terms *angel* and *demon* through a concordance.

3. It has been said that half-truths are like half bricks: they travel further! Transforming himself into an angel of light, Satan uses a barrage of signs, lying wonders, and craftiness to blind people (2 Cor. 11:3, 14; 2 Thess. 2:9). The need to exercise discernment in judging between good and evil is urgent. Are you memorizing, meditating on, and studying the Word of God? If not, you are inviting the deceptive attacks of Satan. A favorite tactic of Satan is to obstruct the gospel by the bad testimony of a Christian. Ask God to help you be a good influence to draw people to Christ at home, work, and school.

2
Fighting the Noble War—Part 2

Outline

Introduction
A. Satan Attacks Sound Doctrine
   1. His attack upon Christ
     a) 1 Timothy 2:5-7
     b) 1 Timothy 3:16
     c) 1 Timothy 6:14-16
   2. His attack upon the gospel
B. Satan Attacks Biblical Morality
   1. 1 Timothy 1
   2. 1 Timothy 2
   3. 1 Timothy 4
   4. 1 Timothy 5
   5. 1 Timothy 6

Lesson
I. Our Responsibility to the Church (v. 18)
  A. A Command to Obey (v. 18*a*)
    1. Duty ignored
    2. Duty illustrated
      a) Paul
      b) The prophets
  B. A Commission to Fulfill (v. 18*b*)
    1. A deposit of truth
    2. The gospel of God
  C. A Confirmation to Honor
    1. Confirmation through the prophets
    2. Confirmation through the elders

II. Our Responsibility to the Lord (v. 19*a*)
   A. An Obligation to Truth
   B. An Obligation to Purity
III. Our Responsibility to the Enemy (v. 19*b*)

Introduction

In 1 Timothy 1:18-20 Paul calls Timothy to be aware that he is in a war: "This charge I commit unto thee, son Timothy, according to the prophecies which pointed to thee, that thou by them mightest war a good warfare, holding faith, and a good conscience, which some, having put away concerning faith, have made shipwreck; of whom are Hymenaeus and Alexander, whom I have delivered unto Satan, that they may learn not to blaspheme."

The key phrase in verse 18 is "war a good warfare" or "fight the noble war." It is a call to fight against the forces of Satan. In addition to speaking of that war in the first chapter of 1 Timothy, Paul mentions it again in the last: "Fight the good fight of faith" (6:12).

Paul outlines Timothy's task in chapter 1. He was to confront the false leaders in the church at Ephesus and surrounding areas. Verses 18-20 are a summary of the task Timothy was to fulfill as a front-line soldier, called to an intense part of the battle. In the church at Ephesus, leaders were functioning as the agents of Satan by sowing false doctrine and living ungodly life-styles.

Basically, then, those were the two issues Timothy had to confront—the attack on sound doctrine and the attack on biblical morality.

   A. Satan Attacks Sound Doctrine

      1. His attack upon Christ

         a) 1 Timothy 2:5-7—"There is one God, and one mediator between God and men, the man, Christ Jesus, who gave himself a ransom for all, to be testified in due time. For this I am ordained a preacher, and an apostle (I speak the truth in Christ, and lie not), a teacher of the Gentiles in faith and verity." Apparently the false leaders in the church were attacking the work of Christ on the cross and His mediatory role.

b) 1 Timothy 3:16—"Without controversy great is the mystery of godliness: God was manifest in the flesh, justified in the Spirit, seen of angels, preached unto the nations, believed on in the world, received up into glory." This verse, which chronicles the life and work of Christ, acknowledges that the mystery of the incarnation is difficult to understand—but is nonetheless.

c) 1 Timothy 6:14-16—"Thou keep this commandment without spot, unrebukeable, until the appearing of our Lord Jesus Christ; which in his times he shall show, who is the blessed and only Potentate, the King of kings, and Lord of lords; who only hath immortality, dwelling in the light which no man can approach unto; whom no man hath seen, nor can see; to whom be honor and power everlasting. Amen." Because the deity of Jesus Christ was apparently being attacked, Paul affirmed that Jesus is God.

2. His attack upon the gospel

a) 1 Timothy 1:4—"Neither give heed to fables and endless genealogies, which minister questions rather than godly edifying which is in faith, so do." Instead of teaching the gospel and true doctrine, these false leaders were teaching fables, Jewish myths, and genealogies. Such issues only raise questions rather than offer answers. They bring no edification because they're not ministering the true faith.

b) 1 Timothy 1:5—"The end of the commandment is love out of a pure heart, and of a good conscience, and of faith unfeigned." The false teachers at Ephesus no doubt were turned aside, swerving from a pure conscience.

c) 1 Timothy 1:7—"Desiring to be teachers of the law, understanding neither what they say, nor that about which they affirm." Along with perverting the gospel, these men also perverted the law of God. While they esteem themselves to be teachers of the law, Paul claims they don't even understand what they were affirming so dogmatically.

d) 1 Timothy 1:15—"This is a faithful saying, and worthy of all acceptance, that Christ Jesus came into the world to save sinners, of whom I am chief." The false teachers at Ephesus were apparently saying that salvation was available to an elite group—not to plain, ordinary sinners.

e) 1 Timothy 1:17—"Unto the King eternal, immortal, invisible, the only wise God, be honor and glory forever and ever. Amen." Again, this affirmation of the true God is given because of an attack against sound doctrine in the church.

f) 1 Timothy 2:3-4—"This is good and acceptable in the sight of God, our Savior, who will have all men to be saved, and to come unto the knowledge of the truth." Perhaps they were denying the availability of salvation for all people.

g) 1 Timothy 4:1-2—"The Spirit speaketh expressly that, in the latter times, some shall depart from the faith, giving heed to seducing spirits, and doctrines of demons, speaking lies in hypocrisy, having their conscience seared with a hot iron." In their hypocrisy these leaders departed from sound teaching.

Repeatedly Timothy was enjoined to preach sound doctrine in an effort to combat unsound teaching that was widespread in the church. False doctrine was being taught by men who had risen to the heights of leadership. These men had all the right credentials but were teaching lies about Christ and His saving gospel.

Ministers of Satan

A series of articles in the *Los Angeles Times* chronicled a meeting of New Testament scholars who assembled to determine the truthfulness of what Jesus said (e.g., John Dart, "Scholars Will Vote on Jesus' Sayings," Saturday, 25 Nov. 1978, sec. 2:25). Even the assertion that such a task is necessary attacks the credibility of the Word of God and the Lord Jesus Christ, which was their intent. Such men masquerade as teachers of the New Testament but don't understand what they teach or the God they speak of. Certainly they have no authority to vote on the veracity of Christ's words. The character of false teachers, elders, pastors, prophets, and apostates is consistent: they attack the person, work, and teaching of the Lord Jesus Christ. That is because they are energized by Satan. Such people are not well-meaning souls who have slipped a little in their understanding; they are agents of Satan.

B. Satan Attacks Biblical Morality

1. 1 Timothy 1—In verse 5 Paul says these men don't have integrity of character. They didn't love out of a pure heart, good conscience, and sincere faith. In verses 9-10 Paul describes the false leaders as being lawless, disobedient, ungodly sinners, unholy, profane murderers of fathers and mothers, man slayers, fornicators, homosexuals, kidnapers, liars, and perjurers. Their morality matched their doctrine. They erred in conduct as well as in theology. In verse 19 Paul says they have become shipwrecked. In verse 20 he says they have blasphemed by speaking evil of the true God.

2. 1 Timothy 2—Women in the Ephesian church had substituted outward adornment for inward godliness (vv. 8-10).

3. 1 Timothy 4—Paul said to Timothy, "Be a good minister of Jesus Christ, nourished up in the words of faith and of good doctrine, unto which thou hast attained. But refuse profane and old wives' fables, and exercise thyself rather unto godliness. For bodily exercise profiteth little, but godliness is profitable unto all things, having promise of the life that now is, and of that which is to come" (vv. 6-8). Preoccupation with the external and the physical should be replaced with exercise that leads to godliness.

4. 1 Timothy 5—Verses 11-13, 15 say, "The younger widows refuse; for when they have begun to grow wanton

against Christ, they will marry, having condemnation, because they have cast off their first faith. And, besides, they learn to be idle, wandering about from house to house; and not only idle but tattlers also, and busybodies, speaking things which they ought not. . . . For some are already turned aside after Satan." Apparently some of the leaders were encouraging such behavior.

5. 1 Timothy 6—Paul condemned leaders who were "proud, knowing nothing, but doting about questions and disputes of words, of which cometh envy, strife, railings, evil suspicions, perverse disputings of men of corrupt minds, and destitute of the truth, supposing that gain is godliness" (vv. 4-5). They had perverted doctrine and purity of life.

Qualifications in Contrast

Timothy was called to confront evil and error in high places. In 1 Timothy 3:1-15 Paul gives biblical qualifications for leadership that are a stark contrast to the character of certain elders at Ephesus. In context, the main purpose of those qualifications is to contrast wrong leadership with right leadership. Although many wanted to be teachers and leaders, only blameless men were to be designated as elders. Apparently Timothy was to confront men who wanted the office but were not level-headed, moderate men, each married to one wife. In 1 Timothy 5:20 Paul says, "Them [elders] that sin rebuke before all, that others also may fear." Those who aren't what they ought to be are to be reprimanded before the whole church. Timothy had a difficult job. He had to discipline false leaders and call the church back to the truth of God's revelation and godly living.

Lesson

In the midst of this fiery conflict Timothy had to understand his responsibility to three things—the church, the Lord, and the blasphemers or enemies themselves. The same is true for all of us.

I. OUR RESPONSIBILITY TO THE CHURCH (v. 18)

"This charge I commit unto thee, son Timothy, according to the prophecies which pointed to thee, that thou by them mightest war a good warfare."

As an apostle in the church, Paul commanded Timothy to carry out the commission given to him by Paul and confirmed by those who had the gift of prophecy. Timothy had a responsibility to those within the church who by the Spirit of God called him into the ministry.

A. A Command to Obey (v. 18a)

"Charge" refers to a military command. It is not something to be discussed but an order to be carried out. Paul was putting Timothy under military obligation.

In 1 Timothy 5:21 he says, "I charge thee before God, and the Lord Jesus Christ, and the elect angels, that thou observe these things without preferring one before another, doing nothing by partiality." Paul used a different term from the one he used in 1:18, but it has the same meaning. However, he used the same term in 1 Timothy 6:13-14: "I command thee in the sight of God, who maketh all things alive, and before Christ Jesus, who before Pontius Pilate witnessed a good confession, that thou keep this commandment without spot, unrebukeable, until the appearing of our Lord Jesus Christ." Paul commanded Timothy as a general would a colonel.

1. Duty ignored

Timothy's responsibility was a duty in every sense of the word. Sadly, many don't understand what that word means anymore. Some Christians would rather talk about freedom, success, joy, peace, and fulfillment. They see spirituality as a means to satisfy their indulgences. They know little about fulfilling their spiritual duty for the glory of God.

2. Duty illustrated

   a) Paul—In Acts 26 Paul says, "O King Agrippa, I was not disobedient unto the heavenly vision" (v. 19). Paul was confronted by the Lord Jesus Christ on the Damascus Road. When He appeared to Paul later on, He commanded him to minister as an apostle to the Gentiles. Paul obeyed. He knew about duty. In 1 Corinthians 9:16 he says, "Woe is unto me, if I preach not the gospel!" Paul had a sense of divine obligation to use his gifts and fulfill his calling.

   b) The prophets—In Exodus 4:1 Moses backs away from his duty as a spokesman for God. Because of that the Lord was angry with him. Also, Isaiah, Jeremiah, Ezekiel, and Jonah had the duty of speaking for God.

   Paul told Timothy, "Preach the word; be diligent in season, out of season" (2 Tim. 4:2). Whether it was welcomed or not, Timothy was to preach the Word of God. Similarly, Ezekiel preached to people who did not want to hear what he had to say. The Lord said to him, "Thou son of man, the children of thy people still are talking against thee by the walls and in the doors of the houses, and speak one to another, every one to his brother, saying, Come, I pray you, and hear what is the word that cometh forth from the Lord" (Ezek. 33:30). The people were ridiculing Ezekiel. Verse 31 says, "They come unto thee as the people come, and they sit before thee as my people, and they hear thy words, but they will not do them; for with their mouth they show much love, but their heart goeth after their covetousness." The people heard what Ezekiel had to say but did not respond because they were distracted by worldly interests. Verse 32 says, "Lo, thou art unto them as a very lovely song of one that hath a very pleasant voice, and can play well on an instrument; for they hear thy words, but they do them not." Ezekiel preached to people who believed he was nothing more than entertainment or a curiosity. Nevertheless, he preached faithfully. Why? Because Ezekiel was under command. He had a duty to fulfill.

That's exactly what Paul was saying to Timothy. There were some in the Ephesian church who didn't listen to Timothy. Similarly, many today won't listen to the Word of God. God said to Isaiah, "Go and tell this people, Hear ye indeed, but understand not; and see ye indeed, but perceive not" (Isa. 6:9). No matter how much you preach, some people will not listen. In fact, preaching has somewhat depreciated today, especially preaching the Bible. The command to Timothy was simple—fight a noble war against the foes of Satan by using the Word of God. The only way to do that is to be "nourished up in the words of faith and of good [sound] doctrine" (1 Tim. 4:6). In spite of how many people shake your hand, say how great you sound, but don't do what you say, don't stop preaching. And command others to fulfill their duty to God.

B. A Commission to Fulfill (v. 18b)

In addition to a command, Paul told Timothy that he had a commission: "I commit unto thee, son Timothy" (v. 18). The Greek word translated "commit" (*paratithēmi*) speaks of a valued deposit that would be kept in a bank.

1. A deposit of truth

What was this deposit that Paul gave to Timothy? A deposit of truth. And truth has supreme value. In 2 Timothy 2:2 Paul says, "The things that thou hast heard from me among many witnesses, the same commit thou to faithful men, who shall be able to teach others also." That which Paul entrusted to Timothy needed to be entrusted to others. Paul repeatedly told Timothy to guard that sacred trust.

2. The gospel of God

In 1 Timothy 1:12 Paul says, "I thank Christ Jesus . . . in that he counted me faithful, putting me into the ministry." The glorious gospel of God was committed to Paul (v. 11). In Galatians 1:12 Paul says, "I neither received it [the gospel] of man, neither was I taught it, but by the revelation of Jesus Christ." Paul took the trust of sound doctrine he received from Jesus and passed it on to Timothy. At the end of 1 Timothy Paul says, "O Timothy, keep that which is committed to thy trust" (6:20). In 2 Timothy 1:14 he says, "That good thing which was committed unto thee keep by the Holy Spirit."

C. A Confirmation to Honor

First Timothy 1:18 tells us that Timothy's command and commission were confirmed through prophecies. God used the gift of prophecy and the office of prophet to speak His will and word to the early church. I and any other minister today have the gift of prophecy only in the sense that we speak forth the Word of God. We are not receiving any new revelation.

1. Confirmation through the prophets

The apostles primarily spoke doctrine. Acts 2:42 refers to "the apostles' doctrine." In slight contrast, Acts 13:1-3; 15:32; 21:9-12; 22:14-15, 21; and 26:16-18 tell of prophets bringing the Word of God to a given situation in the church and applying it in a practical way.

Although we don't know which prophets Paul was referring to in 1 Timothy 1:18 or when the prophecies were given, we do know that there were more than one as Paul used the plural "prophecies." He said those prophecies pointed specifically to Timothy.

2. Confirmation through the elders

The culmination of those prophecies is 1 Timothy 4:14: "Neglect not the gift that is in thee, which was given thee by prophecy, with the laying on of the hands of the presbytery." In other words, God gave that gift to Timothy, articulated it through prophecy, and then confirmed it by the laying on of hands by the elders. The elders confirmed Timothy to the ministry after God had done so by the voice of the prophets. Although we don't know what God said in those prophecies, we know that Paul said to Timothy, "Do the work of an evangelist" (2 Tim. 4:5) and "preach the word" (2 Tim. 4:2).

I wish confirmation of the call to preach was as clear today. Wouldn't it be great if we came together on the Lord's Day and the Spirit of God spoke through one of us directly and pointed out in the congregation who was called to preach? Does the Lord still call men to preach? Yes. He still speaks to the heart, but the call is inaudible. The only way we know whether a man is called or not is to watch his life.

Anyone who serves the Lord Jesus Christ by articulating the truth of God should be confirmed by the church. It affirms that they represent the Lord. In addition, men called to preach should understand that they are called to do their spiritual duty, entrusted with the very Word of the living God.

I find myself in a position similar to that of Timothy. I'm under mandate by God to do my duty. I have been given a tremendous trust through generations of people before me who gave me the truth of God. And I have been confirmed by the church. I remember my ordination well—facing two hundred pastors and answering questions for hour after hour. From that day on I have been committed to fulfill that responsibility as affirmed by the church.

Certainly there are times in the distress of battle when it seems your call is all you have to cling to. You may say, "I'm not happy with the way things are going. I'm weary in the battle. I'm tired of the fight. I'm tired of people who come and listen, yet do nothing about it. I just want a vacation. I want to get out." In times like those you must remember that you're called, you're commissioned, you're commanded, you're confirmed —and you have no choice.

A Man Who Took God Seriously

Commentator William Barclay wrote this about the great Scottish preacher John Knox: "He had been teaching in St. Andrews. His teaching was supposed to be private but many came to it, for he was obviously a man with a message. So the people urged him 'that he would take the preaching place upon him. But he utterly refused, alleging that he would not run where God had not called him. . . . Whereupon they privily among themselves advising, having with them in council Sir David Lindsay of the Mount, they concluded that they would give a charge to the said John, and the publicly by the mouth of their preacher.' "

In other words, these people said Knox should be preaching, not just holding a private Bible study in St. Andrews. Because he wouldn't preach on his own, the church decided to command him publicly.

"Sunday came and Knox was in church and John Rough was preaching. The said John Rough, preacher, directed his words to the said John Knox, saying: 'Brother, ye shall not be offended, albeit that I speak unto you that which I have in charge, even from all those that are here present, which is this: In the name of God, and of his Son Jesus Christ, and in the name of these that presently call you by my mouth, I charge you that you refuse not his holy vocation, but . . . that you take upon you the public office and charge of preaching, even as you look to avoid God's heavy displeasure, and desire that he shall multiply his graces with you.' And in the end he said to those that were present: 'Was not this your charge to me? And do ye not approve this vocation?' They answered: 'It was: and we approve it.' Whereat the said John, abashed, burst forth in most abundant tears, and withdrew himself to his chamber. His countenance and behavior, from that day till the day that he was compelled to present himself to the public place of preaching, did sufficiently declare the grief and trouble of his heart; for no man saw any sign of mirth in him, neither yet had he pleasure to accompany any man, many days together.' " John Knox went into isolation. Deep in sorrow, he was overwhelmed with the duty, commission, and confirmation by the people to preach the Word of God.

Barclay tells us, "John Knox was chosen; he did not want to answer the call; but he had to, for the choice had been made by God. Years afterwards the Regent Morton uttered his famous epitaph by Knox's graveside: 'In respect he bore God's message, to whom he must make account for the same, he (albeit he was weak and an unworthy creature, and a fearful man) feared not the faces of men' " (*The Letters to Timothy, Titus, and Philemon* [Philadelphia: Westminster, 1975], pp. 49-50).

John Knox is an example of the call to Timothy. He illustrates the need to understand one's responsibility to the church when called, commissioned, and confirmed to preach.

II. OUR RESPONSIBILITY TO THE LORD (v. 19*a*)

"Holding faith, and a good conscience."

Elsewhere in this epistle Paul mentions faith and conscience together. In 1:5 he says, "The end of the commandment is love out of a pure heart, and of a good conscience, and of faith unfeigned." In 3:9 he speaks of "holding the mystery of the faith in a pure conscience."

A. An Obligation to Truth

"Holding faith" refers to believing in the truth and holding fast to it. It also refers to the content of faith—*the* faith itself. We could say overall it is a commitment to believe the truth of God.

Throughout this epistle Paul has talked about those who have erred concerning the faith (e.g., 1:6; 6:10, 21). He didn't want Timothy to do that.

B. An Obligation to Purity

A "good conscience" is a conscience that is pure or undefiled. The conscience is the self-judging faculty that helps one discern right from wrong. A good conscience gives a positive evaluation of our lives. It's a conscience "void of offense toward God, and toward men" (Acts 24:16)—a conscience at rest.

Our obligation to God is to uphold the truth and live a pure life. The two key terms in 1 Timothy are doctrine and godliness. Truth and purity, faith and good conscience are different ways of saying the same thing. The call is ever and always to godliness as well as sound doctrine.

III. OUR RESPONSIBILITY TO THE ENEMY (v. 19*b*)

"Which some, having put away concerning faith, have made shipwreck."

In this verse Paul reminds Timothy of the contrast between a good soldier and a bad soldier. It was Timothy's task to identify and confront false leaders in the church at Ephesus.

Bad Roots Grow in Bad Soil

Sound teaching and pure living go together. There is an insepara-
ble link between truth and morality, between right belief and right
behavior. Theological error has its roots more often in moral rather
than intellectual soil. People teach wrong doctrine not because
they lack understanding but because they are evil. Their theology
is constructed to accommodate their fallen nature. Thus false
teachers, liberals, cultists, occultists, and anyone else who teaches
error are not simply misguided, because their hearts are evil (Jer.
17:9). Those who will not submit their evil to the cleansing work of
Christ through the gospel invent a philosophy or teaching that ac-
commodates their evil. The reason theologians are meeting to vote
on what Jesus said is not because they cannot verify the accuracy of
Scripture, but because there are things in the Bible they refuse to
submit to. They seek to eliminate what they refuse to accept. May
God save the church from evil and the corrupt people who teach it.

Focusing on the Facts

1. In the church at Ephesus leaders were functioning as the agents
   of Satan by _____ _____ _____
   and _____ _____ _____ (see pp.
   26-27).
2. The false teachers at Ephesus were apparently saying that salvation was available only to an _____ _____
   (1 Tim. 1:15; see p. 28).
3. Why do people attack the person and work of Christ (see p.
   29)?
4. Even though he was ridiculed, Ezekiel continued to preach.
   Why (see p. 32)?
5. What was the deposit Paul gave to Timothy (see p. 33)?
6. How did God confirm Timothy's call to preach (1 Tim. 1:18;
   4:14; see pp. 34-35)?
7. How does God confirm a man's call to preach today (see p. 35)?
8. What does faith refer to in 1 Timothy 1:19 (see p. 37)?
9. What did Paul mean by a good conscience (1 Tim. 1:19; see p.
   37)?
10. Two key terms in 1 Timothy are _____ and
    _____ (see p. 37).

Pondering the Principles

1. Sin cannot be compartmentalized. If a person has unrighteous thoughts they will be manifested by unrighteous behavior. In 1 Timothy 4:1 Paul says that "some shall depart from the faith." And in the next verse Paul says that such bad theology inevitably leads to godless, hypocritical living. The key to Christlike living is Christlike thinking. That is why Paul told Timothy to be "nourished up in the words of faith and of good doctrine" (1 Tim. 4:6). The best way to understand man is to study man's Creator—God. Begin your spiritual inventory by examining what you think about God. Spiritual growth takes place as we focus our thoughts on God. As we behold Him we are changed into His likeness (2 Cor. 4:3-6).

2. It is imperative that the church has godly leadership. In fact, it has been said that everything rises or falls on leadership. The church is God's holy temple, and "if any man defile the temple of God, him shall God destroy" (1 Cor. 3:17). It is understandable, then, that Paul wanted Timothy to confront the false leadership in Ephesus and establish the godly ones. One factor that contributes to the problem of leadership in the church is applying worldly leadership standards. In 1 Timothy 3 Paul relays God's standard for leadership in the church. Do you desire to have an impact on people's lives, bringing them into greater conformity to Christ? Review the biblical qualifications listed in 1 Timothy 3. Ask the Holy Spirit to give you insight into the aspects of godliness you fall short in.

3
Delivered to Satan—Part 1

Outline

Introduction
A. Defining "Delivered unto Satan"
B. Applying "Delivered unto Satan"
C. Analyzing "Delivered unto Satan"

Lesson
I. Positive Illustrations of Deliverance
  A. Job—An Illustration of Piety
    1. The benefits of piety
    2. The challenges to piety
      a) The first test
        (1) A divine restriction
        (2) A satanic destruction
        (3) A godly reaction
      b) The second test
  B. Jesus—An Illustration of Purity
  C. Paul—An Illustration of Humility
  D. Peter—An Illustration of Stability

Conclusion

Introduction

In 1 Timothy 1:18-20 Paul says, "This charge I commit unto thee, son Timothy, according to the prophecies which pointed to thee, that thou by them mightest war a good warfare, holding faith, and a good conscience, which some, having put away concerning faith, have made shipwreck; of whom are Hymenaeus and Alexander,

41

whom I have delivered unto Satan, that they may learn not to blaspheme."

A. Defining "Delivered unto Satan"

The Greek term translated "delivered" (*paradidōmi*) means "to abandon." It expresses the idea of removing protection—abandoning someone to Satan. The same word is used in Acts 15:26 and is translated "hazarded" in the King James Version. Therefore "delivered" conveys exposure to great danger.

B. Applying "Delivered unto Satan"

Paul uses the same term in 1 Corinthians 5 in reference to a person in the church who was living with "his father's wife" (v. 1). In verse 5 Paul enjoins the church at Corinth to "deliver such a one unto Satan for the destruction of the flesh." In 1 Timothy 1:20 and 1 Corinthians 5:5 we find an explicit command to abandon someone to Satan.

A Rose-Colored Error

Some believers say that a Christian can never be subject to Satan, no matter what the conditions are. Even though that claim is continually repeated, it is not biblical. Not only is it possible for a Christian to be handed over to Satan, but also it is a ministry of the church to do so under certain circumstances. And there are times when God Himself does that very thing.

C. Analyzing "Delivered unto Satan"

A person is turned over to Satan by being put out of the church—disfellowshiped, or in old terminology, excommunicated. Consequently, he is cut off from the fellowship of God's children and the Lord's Table. Matthew 18:15-35 makes clear that when a person claiming to be a believer continues in sin and ignores what the church has to say, he is to be put out of that fellowship and treated as an unbeliever. That places the sinning person under Satan's control. The apostle John said, "The whole world lieth in [the control of] wickedness [lit., "the wicked one"]" (1 John

5:19). The world is already in Satan's hands because of the entrance of sin. The instruction to the church in 1 Timothy 1:20 to turn Hymenaeus and Alexander over to Satan indicates that they were under the umbrella of protection from their association with the church. Since it is the object of God's care, love, and blessing, the church is insulated and protected. The same was true of Israel. There were unbelievers in the community of the redeemed in Israel who by virtue of their association with the people of God were under a certain degree of protection. The church discipline process culminates in putting sinning members out from that protection, leaving them exposed to Satan.

Lesson

I. POSITIVE ILLUSTRATIONS OF DELIVERANCE

We have seen that God will deliver a sinning associate of the redeemed over to Satan, but the following illustrations show that that isn't the only incident when God might choose to do so.

A. Job—An Illustration of Piety

1. The benefits of piety

Chapter 1 introduces Job as a perfect and upright man, fearing God and shunning evil. Verses 2-5 say, "There were born unto him seven sons and three daughters. His substance also was seven thousand sheep, and three thousand camels, and five hundred yoke of oxen, and five hundred she-asses, and a very great household; so that this man was the greatest of all the men of the east. And his sons went and feasted in their houses, every one his day, and sent and called for their three sisters to eat and to drink with them. And it was, when the days of their feasting were finished, that Job sent and sanctified them, and rose up early in the morning, and offered burnt offerings according to the number of them all; for Job said, It may be that my sons have sinned, and cursed God in their hearts. Thus did Job continually."

Because of his spiritual conscientiousness Job kept his heart right before God. In addition, he offered sacrifices for his children on the presumption that in their hearts they may have thought something that was wrong. He wanted to be sure all sin was covered. Indeed, Job was a good man and enjoyed great blessings.

2. The challenges to piety

Job 1:6-8 says, "There was a day when the sons of God [angels] came to present themselves before the Lord, and Satan came also among them. And the Lord said unto Satan, From where comest thou? Then Satan answered the Lord, and said, From going to and fro in the earth, and from walking up and down in it. And the Lord said unto Satan, Hast thou considered my servant, Job, that there is none like him in the earth, a perfect and an upright man, one who feareth God, and shuneth evil?" Since Satan wants to diminish the work of God because of his desire to have greater glory, he replies, "Doth Job fear God for nothing?" (v. 9). He was accusing Job of serving God out of selfish motives. He continues in verse 10, "Hast not thou made an hedge about him, and about his house, and about all that he hath on every side? Thou hast blessed the work of his hands, and his substance is increased in the land." Satan accuses Job of worshiping God because of what he received from God. In verse 11 Satan asserts, "Put forth thine hand now, and touch all that he hath, and he will curse thee to thy face."

a) The first test

(1) A divine restriction

The Lord then replied to Satan, "Behold, all that he hath is in thy power; only upon himself put not forth thine hand. So Satan went forth from the presence of the Lord" (1:12). God turned Job over to Satan. He allowed him to do anything he wanted to Job's possessions but was prohibited from harming Job himself.

(2) A satanic destruction

Job 1:13-16 tells us, "There was a day when his sons and his daughters were eating and drinking wine in their eldest brother's house; and there came a messenger unto Job, and said, The oxen were plowing, and the asses feeding beside them, and the Sabeans fell upon them, and took them away; yea, they have slain the servants with the edge of the sword, and I only am escaped alone to tell thee. While he was yet speaking, there came also another, and said, The fire of God is fallen from heaven, and hath burned up the sheep, and the servants, and consumed them, and I only am escaped alone to tell thee." Satan incited the Sabeans into stealing some of Job's animals and killing his servants. Moreover, he influenced others to start a fire that destroyed Job's crops and sheep. In addition, verse 17 says that the Chaldeans, who were also motivated by Satan, took away his camels (v. 17).

Verses 18-19 reveal the worst news of all: "Thy sons and thy daughters were eating and drinking wine in their eldest brother's house; and, behold, there came a great wind from the wilderness, and smote the four corners of the house, and it fell on the young men, and they are dead, and I only am escaped alone to tell thee." All his crops, all his animals, and all his sons were gone—destroyed by Satan.

(3) A godly reaction

Verses 20-21 say that in response "Job arose, and tore his mantle, and shaved his head, and fell down upon the ground, and worshiped, and said, Naked came I out of my mother's womb, and naked shall I return there. The Lord gave, and the Lord hath taken away; blessed be the name of the Lord." In all that happened, Job did not sin by accusing God because his faith didn't rest on positive circumstances. Although the devil charges that people follow God because of what He gives them, we see here that that is not the case. A truly regenerated person will love God regardless of the circumstances. Using Job as an object lesson, God points out to Satan that true saving faith is unwavering.

One of the central themes of the book of Job is the manifestation of godly character. The godly man loves God and worships Him not because of what He has given but because of who He is.

b) The second test

Satan then returned. Job 2:1-6 says, "Again there was a day when the sons of God came to present themselves before the Lord, and Satan came also. . . . And the Lord said unto Satan . . . Hast thou considered my servant, Job, that there is none like him in the earth, a perfect and an upright man, one that feareth God, and shuneth evil? . . . And Satan answered the Lord, and said, Skin for skin, yea, all that a man hath will he give for his life. But put forth thine hand now, and touch his bone and his flesh, and he will curse thee to thy face. And the Lord said unto Satan, Behold, he is in thine hand; but save his life" (vv. 3-6). God allowed Satan to afflict Job's body but restricted him from taking Job's life. Consequently, Satan left the presence of the Lord and afflicted Job with sores from the soles of his feet to the top of his head (v. 7). Job's wife responded by telling him to curse God, but Job rebuked her, saying, "Shall we receive good at the hand of God, and shall we not receive evil?" Verse 10 concludes, "In all this did not Job sin with his lips."

Chapters 3-10 chronicle Job's sorrow. In 6:2 he laments, "Oh, that my grief were thoroughly weighed, and my calamity laid in the balances together!" In 10:1-2 he says, "My soul is weary of my life. . . . I will say unto God, Do not condemn me; show me why thou contendest with me." Job was confused. He had lost his crops, animals, children, home, and health. However, God did not choose to answer him at that time. It is during this period when God was silent that Job's three friends offered their opinions.

Finally the Lord "answered Job out of the whirlwind" (38:1). But God didn't give Job a full explanation of all the circumstances of his trial. In fact, in all likelihood Job never knew, because many of the events in the first two chapters took place in heaven. Rather, the Lord asked, "Where wast thou when I laid the foundations of the earth?" (38:4). God overwhelmed Job with His omnipotence. That led Job to respond, "I know that thou canst do every thing, and that no thought can be withheld from thee. Who is he who hideth counsel without knowledge? Therefore have I uttered that which I understood not; things too wonderful for me, which I knew not" (42:2-3). In contrition Job concluded, "I have heard of thee by the hearing of the ear, but now mine eye seeth thee. Wherefore I abhor myself, and repent in dust and ashes" (vv. 5-6).

The theme of the book of Job is that genuine godliness does not abandon God under pressure. Job remained faithful, and God rewarded him by restoring his home, crops, and family. Job's trial taught him about God's sovereignty, his own sinfulness, and the necessity of submitting to divine rule no matter what the cost. Job was given over to Satan to glorify God and to show Satan the strength of salvation. Furthermore, within the church of Jesus Christ there are those who, like Job, find themselves in situations that are beyond human understanding. But there's comfort in knowing that God has His holy purposes, and that in His grace a time of restoration and blessing will come.

B. Jesus—An Illustration of Purity

Matthew 4 tells us that God turned over the Lord Jesus Christ Himself to Satan: "Jesus [was] led up by the Spirit into the wilderness to be tested by the devil" (Matt. 4:1). As God put Job in Satan's hands and proved the character of true salvation, so God put His own beloved Son in the hands of Satan to prove His faithfulness. It's for all the world to see that Jesus did not break or waver but stood true as the perfect God-man.

Verse 2 says that Jesus "fasted forty days and forty nights." A comparison of all the gospel records implies that there was temptation throughout that period, but that it reached its peak near the end, when Jesus was particularly vulnerable to temptation.

It has been said that Satan is a pirate who looks to find a vessel that sails without a fleet. Satan attacks people when they are not under the protection of others. Jesus was alone for forty days in a barren place overlooking the Dead Sea. Having been led there by God, Satan comes to Jesus and tempts Him.

The first thing he did was tempt Jesus to eat bread. Then he tempted Him to dive off the Temple and call for a miraculous rescue, thus (presumably) to be hailed as the Messiah. Finally Satan encouraged Jesus to take control of the kingdoms of the world. In each instance Satan's attempts were in areas where Jesus had a right to assert Himself. After all, He created bread, He was the Messiah, and He was the ruler of the world's kingdoms. But in spite of His weakness and isolation the Lord resisted any attempt to move out of step with God's timing and will. Therefore Matthew 4:11 says, "The devil leaveth him, and, behold, angels came and ministered unto him." At the end of that time of testing, God blessed Jesus with the ministry of angels for having passed the test, just as He blessed Job for having passed his test. By His own sovereign design God chose to put His own Son into the hands of Satan to bring Himself greater glory.

C. Paul—An Illustration of Humility

In 2 Corinthians 12:1 Paul says, "It is not expedient for me, doubtless, to glory. I will come to visions and revelations of the Lord." On three occasions Paul had a vision of Jesus Christ risen from the dead. In verses 2-5 he says, "I knew a man in Christ . . . caught up to the third heaven. . . . He was caught up into paradise, and heard unspeakable words, which it is not lawful for a man to utter. Of such an one will I glory; yet of myself I will not glory, but in mine infirmities."

Because of his many successes, visions, and revelations, Paul was tempted to boast. However, Paul said, "Though I would desire to glory, I shall not be a fool; for I will say the truth. But now I forbear, lest any man should think of me above that which he seeth me to be, or that he heareth of me. And lest I should be exalted above measure through the abundance of the revelations, there was given to me a thorn in the flesh, the messenger of Satan to buffet me, lest I should be exalted above measure" (vv. 6-7). God gave Paul a thorn in the flesh to prevent him from being filled with pride. Many people have suggested the identity of Paul's thorn—persecution, his physical appearance, epilepsy, malaria, an eye disease. Whatever it was, I believe God turned Paul over to Satan, who inflicted him with physical pain. God did that so Paul would depend on Him.

The Greek word translated "buffet" is used in Matthew 26:67: "They [members of the Sanhedrin] spat in his [Jesus'] face, and buffeted him; and others smote him with the palms of their hands." The word *buffeted* is derived from a term meaning "knuckles," which refers to bone-crushing blows of the fist. Paul indicated that his thorn in the flesh was pummeling him.

Verse 8 declares that Paul "besought the Lord thrice, that it [the thorn] might depart." God was able to remove it, but He chose not to do so because the thorn prevented Paul from becoming proud. He said, "My grace is sufficient for thee; for my strength is made perfect in weakness." And Paul responded, "Most gladly, therefore, will I rather glory in my infirmities, that the power of Christ may rest upon me" (v. 9). Paul learned to take pleasure in his infirmities when he realized they allowed the power of Christ to be manifested in his life.

D. Peter—An Illustration of Stability

In Luke 22:31 Christ addresses Peter, "Simon, Simon, behold, Satan hath desired to have you, that he may sift you as wheat." His saying "Simon" twice highlights the importance of what He was about to say. Satan desired Peter because he was crucial to the development of the early church. In a similar way he wants us. First Peter 5:8 says that our adversary, "the devil, like a roaring lion walketh about, seeking whom he may devour." If Satan could capture the saved, have them abandon their salvation, and swallow them up in his own evil kingdom, then he could win a victory over God.

But Jesus won't let that happen. In verse 32 He says to Peter, "I have prayed for thee, that thy faith fail not. And when thou art converted [restored after repenting of the sin of denying Christ], strengthen thy brethren." Like Job, Peter was protected by God from complete destruction. Christ gave Satan the freedom to afflict Peter, yet He insured his ultimate return to the faith. Peter was released to Satan to learn how to strengthen others.

Peter boastfully said, "Lord, I am ready to go with thee, both into prison, and to death" (v. 33). In His sovereignty God may take a person and test him as He did Peter. A boastful Christian may find himself out from under the protection of God to learn that he can't stand on his own. Although Peter promised he would remain faithful, he denied Christ three times (vv. 54-61). But Peter returned. Verse 62 says that Peter "went out, and wept bitterly." Therefore, as Christ prophesied, Peter repented and was restored to a right relationship with God.

Conclusion

We have seen that people within the community of believers and under the protection of God may be brought into the dominion of Satan for God's holy purpose and glory. Some are turned over to Satan for refining like Peter. Some are turned over to Satan for greater effectiveness like Paul. Some are turned over to Satan for proving the validity of their faith like Job. But all are turned over to bring greater glory to God.

Focusing on the Facts

1. What does the term *delivered* mean (1 Tim. 1:18-20; Acts 15:26; see p. 42)?
2. Are unbelievers who are a part of the church under God's protection? Explain (see pp. 42-43).
3. According to Satan, why did Job serve God (Job 1:9-10; see p. 44)?
4. What was the first restriction God put on Satan's attack upon Job (Job 1:12; see p. 44)?
5. What truth does Job demonstrate about a truly regenerate person (Job 1:20-21; see pp. 45-46)?
6. How did God change the restriction He placed upon Satan (Job 2:3-6; see p. 46)?
7. Why did God turn Christ over to Satan (see p. 47)?
8. What role did angels play in Christ's temptation (Matt. 4:11; see p. 48)?
9. Why was Paul given a thorn in the flesh (2 Cor. 12:7; see p. 49)?
10. What kept Peter's faith from failing (Luke 22:32; see p. 50)?

Pondering the Principles

1. The Bible promises us that "whom the Lord loveth he chasteneth, and scourgeth every son whom he receiveth" (Heb. 12:6). Whereas from a human perspective pain and suffering are unfavorable experiences, we are assured "that all things work together for good for them that love God, to them who are the called according to his purpose" (Rom. 8:28). In this lesson we learned that all trials have a divine purpose and provision. We also learned that God does not inflict a wound that is deeper than necessary. Although we will never fully understand the mind or purposes of God on this side of eternity, we do know that as His children we are not victims of chance. Rather, God gives and withholds so that His strength will be displayed in our weaknesses. Do you despise your frailties? Or like Paul do you glory in your infirmities (2 Cor. 12:10)?

2. Satan is a defeated foe. In the book of Job we're given insight into the limitations of Satan's power. Satan touched Job only to the degree that God allowed him. In fact, God uses Satan to ac-

complish His purposes. That is reminiscent of Joseph's words to his brothers, "Ye thought evil against me; but God meant it unto good" (Gen. 50:20). The belief that God and Satan are two opposite but equal forces is not biblical—they are opposite but not equal. Certainly Scripture teaches that Satan is the "prince of the power of the air" (Eph. 2:2), but at the same time we are assured that his kingdom is ultimately under God's dominion. Indeed, our Father is all-powerful. Are you struggling with hardships that appear insurmountable? Perhaps your God is too small.

4

Delivered to Satan—Part 2

Outline

Introduction

Review
I. Positive Illustrations of Deliverance
   A. Job—An Illustration of Piety
   B. Jesus—An Illustration of Purity
   C. Paul—An Illustration of Humility
   D. Peter—An Illustration of Stability

Lesson
   E. Believers in the Tribulation—An Illustration of Steadfast-ness
   F. Believers in Smyrna—An Illustration of Faithfulness
II. Negative Illustrations of Deliverance
   A. Saul
      1. The meaning of Saul's torment
      2. The cause of Saul's torment
      3. The manifestation of Saul's torment
      4. The product of Saul's torment
   B. Judas
   C. Ananias and Sapphira
   D. The Corinthian Offender
      1. The offense described
      2. The offense corrected
         a) An explanation of the correction
         b) A restriction on the correction
   E. The Church in Thyatira

III. An Examination of Deliverance in 1 Timothy
   A. The Position of Hymenaeus and Alexander in the Church
   B. The Punishment of Hymenaeus and Alexander by the Church

Conclusion

Introduction

In our last lesson we learned that before a person is turned over to Satan, he is under God's protection. Allow me to explain further. Unredeemed humanity as a whole is fallen and in sin. First John 5:19 tells us, "The whole world lieth in wickedness." Furthermore, Romans 1:18-32 says that because man has fallen into sin, God has given him up. Three times the text says that God gave man over to a reprobate mind to work all forms of evil. God abandoned the human race to the power of Satan because of man's sin. Similarly, Ephesians 2:2 says that all unredeemed people live "according to the course of this world, according to the prince of the power of the air, the spirit that now worketh in the sons of disobedience." Unredeemed man is exposed to Satan's power.

Therefore who are the people that God turns over to Satan? They must be those who at one time were not fully exposed to Satan's power. As we have already learned, anyone who is associated with the redeemed community, even an unbeliever, is under God's protection by virtue of that association. For instance, Paul said, "The unbelieving husband is sanctified by the wife" (1 Cor. 7:14). To be identified with the redeemed community is to find a haven from the full fury of Satan. Being delivered to Satan results when God takes a believer or an unbeliever associated with the redeemed and pushes him from the protection of the church into the realm of Satan.

In 1 Timothy 1 Paul instructs Timothy that he must turn over to Satan certain people in the church at Ephesus. Paul set the example for Timothy by putting out Hymenaeus and Alexander "that they may learn not to blaspheme" (v. 20). We must follow that pattern exemplified and taught by Paul.

Review

I. POSITIVE ILLUSTRATIONS OF DELIVERANCE

A. Job—An Illustration of Piety (see pp. 43-47)

Job was more than just a good man; he was the best of men, an upright man who honored God with his life. Nevertheless, Scripture tells us that Job was delivered to Satan. Satan was allowed to destroy Job's family and possessions and bring a terrible illness upon him.

B. Jesus—An Illustration of Purity (see pp. 47-48)

Jesus was led into the wilderness by the Holy Spirit to be tempted by the devil (Matt 4:1-11). That turned out to be a demonstration of Jesus' perfection.

C. Paul—An Illustration of Humility (see pp. 48-49)

God delivered Paul over to Satan resulting in a thorn in the flesh—a physical problem that kept Paul humble and dependent on God.

D. Peter—An Illustration of Stability (see pp. 49-50)

The last person we studied in our previous lesson was Peter. Jesus says to him in Luke 22:31, "Satan hath desired to have you, that he may sift you as wheat." Perhaps Satan had come to God as he did with Job, asking for permission to afflict Peter. Whatever the case, Peter was turned over to Satan so he could strengthen others who would go through severe troubles.

Lesson

E. Believers in the Tribulation—An Illustration of Steadfastness

In Matthew 24 Christ says, "There shall be great tribulation, such as was not since the beginning of the world to this time, no, nor ever shall be. And except those days should be shortened, there should no flesh be saved; but for the elect's sake those days shall be shortened" (vv. 21-22). Believers who will be martyred during that time will cry out "with a loud voice, saying, How long, O Lord, holy and true, dost thou not judge and avenge our blood on them that dwell on the earth?" (Rev. 6:10).

Revelation 7 pictures those martyred saints during the Tribulation. They are standing "before the throne, and before the Lamb, clothed with white robes, and palms in their hands, and [crying] with a loud voice, saying, Salvation to our God who sitteth upon the throne, and unto the Lamb" (vv. 9-10). I believe John is picturing a whole generation of believers who will be turned over to Satan in the Tribulation. However, in the end God will receive praise from those who suffered because of the greatness of their deliverance.

F. Believers in Smyrna—An Illustration of Faithfulness

John recorded a message from Christ to the church in Smyrna: "I know thy works, and tribulation, and poverty (but thou art rich); and I know the blasphemy of them who say they are Jews, and are not, but are the synagogue of Satan. Fear none of those things which thou shalt suffer. Behold, the devil shall cast some of you into prison, that ye may be tried, and ye shall have tribulation ten days; be thou faithful unto death, and I will give thee a crown of life" (Rev. 2:9-10).

The believers at Smyrna were persecuted for their faith. Some were persecuted by the devil to the point of death. God rewarded those faithful believers who were delivered to Satan with a crown of life.

Believers can be delivered to Satan for physical problems, family problems, and even unto death—all for divine purposes.

II. NEGATIVE ILLUSTRATIONS OF DELIVERANCE

I want us to look at the negative aspect of being delivered to Satan because that is the issue in 1 Timothy 1. Hymenaeus and Alexander were not delivered to Satan to prove the validity of their faith, to maintain humility, to strengthen others, to receive a crown of life, or to give praise to God for bringing them through a terrible tribulation. Rather, they were turned over to Satan to be judged by God. The same is true with the following.

A. Saul

In 1 Samuel 16 Samuel examines Jesse's sons because the Lord told him that one of them would be the next king of Israel (v. 1). After realizing that God had not chosen any of his first seven sons, Samuel asked Jesse to bring in his youngest son, David. Verses 12-14 say that Jesse "sent, and brought him in. Now he was ruddy, and of a beautiful countenance, and handsome. And the Lord said, Arise, anoint him; for this is he. Then Samuel took the horn of oil, and anointed him in the midst of his brethren; and the Spirit of the Lord came upon David from that day onward. So Samuel rose up, and went to Ramah. But the Spirit of the Lord departed from Saul, and an evil spirit from the Lord troubled him."

1. The meaning of Saul's torment

Some find it difficult to believe that an evil spirit could come from God. However, we must understand that this passage doesn't say the Lord is evil. And it doesn't mean that an evil spirit dwells in the presence of the Lord. Rather, it means that the demons can't function unless the Lord allows it. When the Spirit of the Lord departed from Saul, it was as if God turned him over to Satan. That allowed Satan to dispatch a demon to torment Saul. The Hebrew term translated "troubled" in verse 14 means "to terrify" or "to torment."

2. The cause of Saul's torment

The Spirit of the Lord empowered Saul to rule as king over Israel. Even so, he was given to rash judgments. His decisions were particularly bad when he was under pressure. On one occasion Saul's impetuousness almost led to the execution of his son for eating honey. He despised the authority of Samuel. His pride led him to pursue dictatorial rule and full devotion from all the people rather than share the glory with anyone. He took the role of a priest and tried to hide his disobedience under a cloak of spirituality. He was a wicked man. So the Spirit of the Lord left Saul and an evil spirit came to terrorize him until his death.

3. The manifestation of Saul's torment

First Samuel 18:5-7 says, "David went out wherever Saul sent him, and behaved himself wisely; and Saul set him over the men of war, and he was accepted in the sight of all the people, and also in the sight of Saul's servants. And it came to pass as they [David and the men of war] came, when David was returned from the slaughter of the Philistine [Goliath], that the women came out of all cities of Israel, singing and dancing, to meet King Saul, with timbrels, with joy, and with instruments of music. And the women spoke to one another as they played, and said, Saul hath slain his thousands, and David his ten thousands."

Because of his pride, "Saul was very angry, and the saying displeased him; and he said, They have ascribed unto David ten thousands, and to me they have ascribed but thousands; and what can he have more, but the kingdom? And Saul watched enviously David, from that day and onward. And it came to pass on the next day, that the evil spirit from God came upon Saul, and he prophesied in the midst of the house; and David [who had become a harpist in Saul's court] played with his hand, as at other times; and there was a javelin in Saul's hand. And Saul cast the javelin; for he said, I will smite David even to the wall with it. And David escaped from his presence twice" (vv. 8-11).

After another victory over the Philistines, David escaped from a third murder attempt by Saul: "The evil spirit from the Lord was upon Saul, as he sat in his house with his javelin in his hand; and David played with his hand. And Saul sought to smite David even to the wall with the javelin, but he slipped away out of Saul's presence; and he smote the javelin into the wall.

58

And David fled, and escaped that night" (1 Sam. 19:9-10).

4. The product of Saul's torment

Saul was terrorized by a demon. And the story of Saul goes from bad to worse. He had been given the Spirit of the Lord and was part of the covenant people of God. But the Spirit of the Lord departed from him, and he was thrust into the kingdom of Satan. Being subject to the control of supernatural evil power lead him to insanity, mass murder, the occult, and ultimately suicide. Puritan Thomas Manton, editor of *The Spiritual Warfare* (Edinburgh: G. Swinton & J. Glen, 1672), observed that the devil delights to vex men with unreasonable terrors—he both tempts and troubles. Although the Spirit of the Lord came back to him temporarily, Saul was so out of control that he stripped himself naked and fell to the floor, humiliating himself (1 Sam. 19:22-24). Later he massacred a group of priests because they had given provisions to David (1 Sam. 22:6-19). Near the end of his life Saul consulted a medium to speak with the dead (1 Sam. 28:7-20). Then he committed suicide in the heat of battle (1 Sam. 31:1-5).

B. Judas

John 13:27 says, "After the sop Satan entered into him [Judas Iscariot]." Christ was with His disciples in the upper room on the night of His betrayal. Judas had been with Jesus for three years. He had seen everything Christ did and heard everything He said. He knew the perfection and power of Christ. Yet Judas rejected all that.

Therefore God turned Judas over to Satan. As part of the community of apostles he had been insulated from the full fury of Satan. But now he was no longer a part of that group. The parallel passage in Luke says, "Then entered Satan into Judas, surnamed Iscariot, being of the number of the twelve. And he went his way, and conferred with the chief priests and captains, how he might betray him unto them. And they were glad, and covenanted to give him money" (22:3-5).

Energized by Satan, Judas sold out Jesus Christ. Then in remorse he put a noose around his neck and hanged himself. Either the rope or the branch snapped, causing his body to fall on a rock and then into a field. Like Saul, Judas committed suicide.

C. Ananias and Sapphira

Acts 5:1 says that "Ananias, with Sapphira, his wife, sold a possession." They had promised the Lord they would give Him all the proceeds from the sale. But they kept back part of the profit, in essence lying to the Holy Spirit. They laid what they claimed to be the entire price at the apostles' feet. The Holy Spirit instructed Peter of their lie. In verse 3 he says to Ananias, "Why hath Satan filled thine heart to lie to the Holy Spirit, and to keep back part of the price of the land?" Ananias lied to the Spirit of God.

Verse 5 records the result of his lie: "Ananias, hearing these words, fell down, and died; and great fear came on all them that heard these things." I believe the Lord turned him over to Satan who filled his heart with deceit and then killed him. Verses 7-11 say, "About the space of three hours after, when his wife, not knowing what was done, came in. . . . Peter said unto her, How is it that ye have agreed together to test the Spirit of the Lord? Behold, the feet of them who have buried thy husband are at the door, and shall carry thee out. Then fell she down immediately at his feet, and died; and the young men came in, found her dead, and, carrying her forth, buried her by her husband. And great fear came upon all the church, and upon as many as heard these things."

Here were two believers who lied to the Holy Spirit. They were turned over to Satan, and he killed them. According to Hebrews 2:14 Satan has power to kill, and there are times when God allows him to use that power. Even a believing couple may be turned over to Satan if they persist in sin. In the case of Ananias and Sapphira God's purpose was not remedial. God turned them over to Satan for judgment.

D. The Corinthian Offender

First Corinthians 5 is another instance of a person's being turned over to Satan. Paul said, "It is reported commonly that there is fornication among you, and such fornication as is not so much as named among the Gentiles, that one should have his father's wife" (v. 1).

1. The offense described

That the word *fornication* is used rather than the word *adultery* leads us to believe this was something done outside of marriage since the Bible uses "adultery" to address sexual immorality within marital bounds. "Father's wife" may indicate that the woman was his stepmother and not his mother, otherwise Paul would have used the word *mother*. So possibly the situation involves a son who started a sexual relationship with his stepmother. Perhaps the marriage between his father and stepmother ended in divorce, but the immoral relationship between the son and the stepmother was still continuing.

However, instead of the Corinthian believers mourning or doing something about it, they were actually proud of the situation (v. 2). Paul responded with the admonition, "Deliver such an one unto Satan for the destruction of the flesh, that the spirit may be saved in the day of the Lord Jesus" (v. 5). Paul wanted the offender to be put out of the church. First Corinthians 5 and 1 Timothy 1:20 are the only places where the terminology of delivering a person to Satan is used. Both places speak of putting the guilty one out of the church, stripping him of the protection of the Body of Christ.

Matthew 18:17 says that the last step in the disciplinary process is to treat the offender as a "heathen man and a tax collector." Likewise, 2 Thessalonians 3 says, "Withdraw yourselves from every brother that walketh disorderly. . . . If any man obey not our word by this epistle, note that man, and have no company with him, that he may be ashamed" (vv. 6, 14). Rather than putting the offender out, the Corinthians boasted about him. Paul said to them, "Your glorying is not good. Know ye not that a little leaven leaveneth the whole lump? Purge out, therefore, the old leaven, that ye may be a new lump, as ye are unleavened" (1 Cor. 5:6-7).

Divine Purification

Through the years I have noticed that there are some people the Lord puts out of the church without us being aware of it. Often they will withdraw from church involvement, and no one knows why. Later we may hear that their lives are in shambles, marred by broken marriages, immorality, or drunkenness. Then we realize that what we didn't know God knew. What we couldn't purge God purged. Paul commanded the church to cast out sinning members because a little leaven leavens the whole lump. Sin can't be allowed to remain in the church.

2. The offense corrected

   a) An explanation of the correction

   Paul said to the Corinthian believers, "I wrote unto you in an epistle not to company with fornicators; not altogether with the fornicators of this world, or with the covetous, or extortioners, or with idolaters, for then must ye needs go out of the world. . . . Therefore, put away from among yourselves that wicked person" (1 Cor. 5:9-10, 13). Why must the church put such a person out of its fellowship? Verse 5 says, "To deliver such an one unto Satan for the destruction of the flesh, that the spirit may be saved in the day of the Lord Jesus." When a person is delivered to Satan, it is for the destruction of his flesh. That refers to judgment, including the possibility of physical death.

   b) A restriction on the correction

   Notice the destruction is limited, as it was on Job, Paul, and Peter. God gave Satan the freedom to destroy the offender's body, but his spirit was to be saved. Evidently the offender was reputed to be a believer because Paul says in verse 11 he was "called a brother." If in fact he was a Christian, Satan would

62

not be able to destroy his spirit even though he could devastate his life.

E. The Church in Thyatira

Another passage that illustrates the devastation of being turned over to Satan is in Revelation 2. Christ said to the church at Thyatira, "I know thy works, and love, and service, and faith, and thy patience, and thy works; and the last to be more that the first. Notwithstanding, I have a few things against thee, because thou allowest that woman, Jezebel, who calleth herself a prophetess, to teach and to seduce my servants to commit fornication, and to eat things sacrificed unto idols" (vv. 19-20).

Speaking of the woman known as Jezebel, Christ said, "I gave her space to repent of her fornication, and she repented not. Behold, I will cast her into a bed, and them that commit adultery with her into great tribulation, except they repent of their deeds" (vv. 21-22). What began as doctrinal deviation led to immorality. Then because the situation was left unchecked, children in the church began to die. Christ promises in verse 23, "I will kill her children with death; and all the churches shall know that I am he who searcheth the minds and hearts; and I will give unto every one of you according to your works." Christ said to the true believers, "As many as have not this doctrine, and who have not known the depths of Satan, as they speak, I will put upon you no other burden" (v. 24).

Some people come to church for the wrong reason. They don't come to submit to Christ as their Savior and Lord but for the benefit they believe comes from associating with a church. Such people are in danger of being turned over to Satan. Furthermore, believers must be cautious not to cultivate disobedience, false doctrine, or immorality. Otherwise, they too may be turned over to Satan for chastening. It is a fearful thing to be turned over to the consuming power that Peter described as a roaring lion (1 Pet. 5:8).

III. AN EXAMINATION OF DELIVERANCE IN 1 TIMOTHY

In 1 Timothy 1:20 Paul says he had delivered Hymenaeus and Alexander to Satan so that they would learn not to blaspheme.

The text does not tell us if this deliverance led to death. Possibly their judgment was disease or devastation of their possessions. We don't know. However, we do know whatever devastation Satan brought was within God's allowance.

As we discussed in chapter 2 (see pp. 26-38), Paul told Timothy that he had a responsibility to the church (v. 18), to the Lord (v. 19a), and to the enemy (v. 19b). Timothy needed to follow Paul's example by dealing with anyone who corrupted the church with false doctrine and unholiness.

A. The Position of Hymenaeus and Alexander in the Church

The agitators Paul refers to as "some" in verse 19 are the same people he spoke of in verses 3, 6, and 7. They were leaders in the church at Ephesus and perhaps in the surrounding churches. Verse 19 indicates that they weren't concerned about having a good conscience, a reminder that bad theology rises out of bad morals. They had rejected the Word of God for a system that would allow them to continue in sin. In fact, Paul said those false leaders "put away" matters of faith (v. 19). The Greek word for "put away" (apotithēmi) means "to violently reject" or "to disregard aggressively." They didn't want anything to do with a pure conscience. Rather, they wanted to live for their own lust, success, and gratification. As a result they were made shipwreck (v. 19). It's like throwing away the rudder and being at the mercy of the wind and sea. Although they confessed to be Christians, they were devoid of any truth because truth doesn't rise out of an immoral heart.

In 2 Timothy 2 we find again that an evil conscience and doctrinal error go together. Verse 17 says that the words of Hymenaeus and another companion, Philetus, "eat as doth a gangrene." Their words were fatal because they erred from the truth. Therefore Paul commanded, "Let everyone that nameth the name of Christ depart from iniquity" (v. 19).

B. The Punishment of Hymenaeus and Alexander by the Church

If Timothy was going to be a good soldier in the noble warfare, he had to deal with the enemy. Paul said of Hymenaeus and Alexander, "I have delivered [them] unto Satan" (1 Tim. 1:20). Paul put those sinning leaders outside the protection of the fellowship into the domain of the devil. He did that so they might "learn" (v. 20). The term *paideuō* in the Greek text speaks of training through punishment. It is used in Luke 23:16, 22, where it speaks of Christ's scourgings and is translated "chastise." The term appears in 1 Corinthians 11:32 and refers to the judgment of sickness and death brought upon those who abused the Lord's Table. We find the same usage in 2 Corinthians 6:9 and Hebrews 12:6-7, 10. In every case the term speaks of chastening through suffering.

Hymenaeus and Alexander were turned over to Satan to learn not to blaspheme, which means to slander God (cf. James 2:7; 2 Tim. 3:2). They had blasphemed God by their disobedience and unholy living and needed to be taught through physically inflicted punishment.

Conclusion

By God's sovereign design certain people are delivered to Satan for either positive or negative purposes. Job, Christ, Paul, Peter, and the believers at Smyrna were delivered to Satan to magnify God. Saul, Judas, Ananias and Sapphira, the Corinthian offender, the Thyatirans, and Hymenaeus and Alexander were delivered to Satan to be chastened. We have seen that such chastening may be physical affliction or sometimes even death.

How do you avoid chastening and judgment? By receiving the truth and reflecting the holiness of Christ. That is the ultimate message behind our text. It may be that God wants to turn you or me over to Satan. If so, my only prayer is that it will be for His glory and our good. If we are delivered, we want it to be for strengthening and advancing His kingdom, not for chastening.

Focusing on the Facts

1. Why will the praise of the saints martyred during the Tribulation exceed that of all the redeemed (see p. 56)?

2. Who allowed Satan to kill some of the believers at Smyrna (see p. 56)?
3. The evil spirit troubling Saul was what (see p. 57)?
4. How did the evil spirit lead Saul to respond to David (1 Sam. 18:8-11; 19:9-10; see p. 58)?
5. Once under the control of demons, whom did Saul turn to for guidance (1 Sam. 28:7-20; see p. 59)?
6. Did God have a remedial purpose for turning Ananias and Sapphira over to Satan? Explain (see p. 60).
7. Explain how fornication differs from adultery (see p. 61)?
8. What does delivered to Satan mean in 1 Corinthians 5:5 (see p. 61)?
9. What restriction did God put on the affliction given to the Corinthian offender (1 Cor. 5:5; see pp. 62-63)?
10. In what final form did God's judgment come to the church in Thyatira (Rev. 2:23; see p. 63)?
11. Who are the people represented by the term *some* in 1 Timothy 1:19 (see p. 64)?
12. What does 2 Timothy 2:19 teach us about the relationship between doctrine and morals (see p. 64)?

Pondering the Principles

1. Most of us understand the need to confront error. And from our study of 1 Timothy 1:18-20, we know in part what the Bible says about it. Yet in our humanness we sometimes find confrontation difficult. Apparently so did Timothy. However, he was blessed with the encouragement and support of a godly mentor—Paul. God has designed us to require the fellowship of other believers (1 Cor. 12:12-26; Eph. 4:11-16). Interdependence is particularly necessary when we are called to battle evil. Be sure you are meeting regularly with other Christians and developing friendships that involve mutual accountability.

2. The problem of evil is a major cause for the rejection of God. How can a good, omnipotent God allow evil to exist? God's goodness means He desires to eliminate evil. God's omnipotence means He has the power to do so. Yet evil continues to exist. The supposed dilemma is that either God is not good or He is not omnipotent—but He can't be both. One fallacy of such reasoning is an improper understanding of what is in fact evil. If evil lacks any eternal purpose, God is indeed less than good.

But if we focus on the fact that God uses suffering to strengthen His children and to magnify His glory, we see that God is both good and omnipotent. We slander God because we lack understanding. To gain further understanding on this important topic, read Norman L. Geisler's *The Roots of Evil* (Grand Rapids: Zondervan, 1978), and take advantage of his helpful bibliography.

Scripture Index

Topical Index

Moody Press, a ministry of the Moody Bible Institute, is designed for education, evangelization, and edification. If we may assist you in knowing more about Christ and the Christian life, please write us without obligation: Moody Press, c/o MLM, Chicago, Illinois 60610.